BIBLE

POCKET BIBLE

on Finances

Scriptures to Renew Your Mind
And Change Your Life

Harrison House
Tulsa, Oklahoma

15 14 13 12 5 4 3 2 1
The Pocket Bible on Finances
ISBN: 978-1-60683-681-1
Copyright © 1995, 2003, 2012 by Harrison House, LLC.
Tulsa, OK 74145

Introduction

This is a time, as never before, to be hooked into God's economic system. While God's financial principles for a stable economy do not fluctuate, the world's economic system changes from day to day.

With God's principles, it is possible to reap a hundredfold return on your giving into His Kingdom, even in the midst of a natural famine, just as Isaac experienced. (Genesis 26:12.) It is possible to remain blessed in the midst of a world economy that is in great turmoil.

The financial principles presented in the Old and New Testament accounts contained in this book, *The Pocket Bible on Finances*, will strengthen your knowledge of God's principles for being a part of a flourishing economy. These principles will guide you into the increase God has planned for your life. They will serve as a guide in all of your financial affairs, enabling you to represent Jesus with highest integrity.

The key to success in every area of your life – including finances, which is our focus in this book – is found in Joshua 1:8 NLT.

"Study this Book of Instruction continually. Mediate on it day and night so you will be sure to obey everything written in it. Only then will you prosper and succeed in all you do.

Opportunity awaits you to step into a higher level of financial responsibility, integrity, and abundance as you meditate continually on the scriptures in this book.

PRAYER

Heavenly Father, thank You for Your guidance in directing me to new financial goals for increase, investing and giving of tithes, offerings, and alms, in Jesus' name.

Thank You that a spirit of wisdom and understanding, counsel and might and knowledge and reverential fear of You, Lord, guide me in all of my financial affairs (Isaiah 11:2).

Thank You, Lord, that Your Spirit causes me to be bold as a lion (Proverbs 28:1) in obeying Your directives so that I can receive the release of wealth that You desire to entrust to me.

Father, thank You for Your Word, which renews my mind from a poverty mentality to one of unlimited abundance. I receive Your will for my life in every area, Lord, which is life more abundantly (John 10:10) and unlimited prosperity in my spirit, soul (which includes the mind, will and emotions), and body (3 John 2).

Because I am seeking first Your Kingdom and Your righteousness, Lord, all of the things which I need are added unto me (Matthew 6:33).

Thank You, Lord, that not only are my needs met, but I am a recipient of the wealth of the wicked (Proverbs 13:22) in this very hour so that I can be a major contributor to the evangelization of the world – bringing Your message of saving grace, healing, deliverance, restoration, preservation, and soundness to others.

Thank You for being faithful to all of the promises of Your Word, Father, in Jesus' name. Amen.

OLD TESTAMENT

While the earth remains, seedtime and harvest, cold and heat, winter and summer, and day and night shall not cease.

Genesis 8:22 NKJV

And God blessed Noah and his sons, and said unto them, Be fruitful, and multiply, and replenish the earth.

Genesis 9:1

I will make you into a great nation, and I will bless you; I will make your name great, and you will be a blessing.

I will bless those who bless you, and whoever

curses you I will curse; and all peoples on earth will be blessed through you.

Genesis 12:2-3 NIV

Then Melchizedek king of Salem brought out bread and wine. He was priest of God Most High, and he blessed Abram, saying,

"Blessed be Abram by God Most High, Creator of heaven and earth. And praise be to God Most High, who delivered your enemies into your hand."

Then Abram gave him a tenth of everything.

The king of Sodom said to Abram, "Give me the people and keep the goods for yourself."

But Abram said to the king of Sodom, "With raised hand I have sworn an oath to the Lord,

God Most High, Creator of heaven and earth, that I will accept nothing belonging to you, not even a thread or the strap of a sandal, so that you will never be able to say, 'I made Abram rich.' I will accept nothing but what my men have eaten and the share that belongs to the men who went with me—to Aner, Eshkol and Mamre. Let them have their share."

Genesis 14:18-24 NIV

When Abram was ninety-nine years old, the Lord appeared to him and said, "I am God Almighty. Obey me and do what is right. I will make an agreement between us, and I will make you the ancestor of many people."

Then Abram bowed facedown on the ground. God said to him, "I am making my agreement with you: I will make you the father of many nations. I am changing your name from Abram to Abraham because I am making you a father of many nations. I will give you many descendants. New nations will be born from you, and kings will come from you. And I will make an agreement between me and you and all your descendants from now on: I will be your God and the God of all your descendants."

Genesis 17:1-7 NCV

And God said unto Abraham, As for Sarai thy wife, thou shalt not call her name Sarai, but Sarah shall her name be.

And I will bless her, and give thee a son also of her: yea, I will bless her, and she shall be a mother of nations; kings of people shall be of her.

Genesis 17:15-16

And the Lord said, Shall I hide from Abraham that thing which I do; Seeing that Abraham shall surely become a great and mighty nation, and all the nations of the earth shall be blessed in him?

For I know him, that he will command his

children and his household after him, and they shall keep the way of the Lord, to do justice and judgment; that the Lord may bring upon Abraham that which he hath spoken of him.

Genesis 18:17-19

Then the angel of the Lord called to Abraham a second time from heaven, and said, "By Myself I have sworn, declares the LORD, because you have done this thing and have not withheld your son, your only son, indeed I will greatly bless you, and I will greatly multiply your seed as the stars of the heavens and as the sand which is on

the seashore; and your seed shall possess the gate of their enemies. In your seed all the nations of the earth shall be blessed, because you have obeyed My voice."

Genesis 22:15-18 NASB

Abraham was now very old, and the Lord had blessed him in every way.

Genesis 24:1 NIV

Now there was a famine in the land—besides the previous famine in Abraham's time—and Isaac went to Abimelek king of the Philistines in Gerar.

The Lord appeared to Isaac and said, "Do not go down to Egypt; live in the land where I tell you to live. Stay in this land for a while, and I will be with you and will bless you. For to you and your descendants I will give all these lands and will confirm the oath I swore to your father Abraham.

"I will make your descendants as numerous as the stars in the sky and will give them all these lands, and through your offspring all nations on earth will be blessed, because Abraham obeyed me and did everything I required of him, keeping my commands, my decrees and my instructions."

Genesis 26:1-5 NIV

Then Isaac sowed in that land, and reaped in the same year a hundredfold; and the Lord blessed him. The man began to prosper, and continued prospering until he became very prosperous; for he had possessions of flocks and possessions of herds and a great number of servants. So the Philistines envied him.

Genesis 26:12-14 NKJV

The Lord appeared to him on the night of his arrival. "I am the God of your father, Abraham," he said. "Do not be afraid, for I am with you and will bless you. I will multiply your descendants, and they will become a great nation. I will do this because of my promise to Abraham, my servant."

Genesis 26:24 NLT

May God Almighty bless you and give you many children. And may your descendants multiply and become many nations!

Genesis 28:3 NLT

Thus the man became exceedingly prosperous, and had large flocks, female and male servants, and camels and donkeys.

Genesis 30:43 NKJV

Joseph is a fruitful vine, a fruitful vine near a spring, whose branches climb over a wall. With bitterness archers attacked him; they shot at him with hostility.

But his bow remained steady, his strong arms

POCKET BIBLE

stayed limber, because of the hand of the Mighty One of Jacob, because of the Shepherd, the Rock of Israel, because of your father's God, who helps you, because of the Almighty, who blesses you with blessings of the skies above, blessings of the deep springs below, blessings of the breast and womb.

Your father's blessings are greater than the blessings of the ancient mountains, than the bounty of the age-old hills. Let all these rest on the head of Joseph, on the brow of the prince among his brothers.

Genesis 49:22-26 NIV

And the Lord said, I have surely seen the affliction of my people which are in Egypt, and have heard their cry by reason of their taskmasters; for I know their sorrows;

And I am come down to deliver them out of

the hand of the Egyptians, and to bring them up out of that land unto a good land and a large, unto a land flowing with milk and honey.

Exodus 3:7-8

And ye shall serve the Lord your God, and he shall bless thy bread, and thy water

Exodus 23:25a

"And Bezalel and Aholiab, and every gifted artisan in whom the Lord has put wisdom and understanding, to know how to do all manner of work for the service of the sanctuary, shall do according to all that the Lord has commanded."

Then Moses called Bezalel and Aholiab, and every gifted artisan in whose heart the Lord had put wisdom, everyone whose heart was stirred, to come and do the work. And they received from Moses all the offering which the children of

Israel had brought for the work of the service of making the sanctuary. So they continued bringing to him free will offerings every morning. Then all the craftsmen who were doing all the work of the sanctuary came, each from the work he was doing, and they spoke to Moses, saying, "The people bring much more than enough for the service of the work which the Lord commanded us to do."

So Moses gave a commandment, and they caused it to be proclaimed throughout the camp, saying, "Let neither man nor woman do any more work for the offering of the sanctuary." And the people were restrained from bringing, for the material they had was sufficient for all the work to be done—indeed too much.

Exodus 36:1-7 NKJV

If you walk in My statutes and keep My commandments so as to carry them out, then I shall give you rains in their season, so that the land will yield its produce and the trees of the field will bear their fruit.

Indeed, your threshing will last for you until grape gathering, and grape gathering will last until sowing time. You will thus eat your food to the full and live securely in your land. I shall also grant peace in the land, so that you may lie down with no one making you tremble. I shall also eliminate harmful beasts from the land, and no sword will pass through your land.

But you will chase your enemies and they will fall before you by the sword; five of you will chase a hundred, and a hundred of you will chase ten thousand, and your enemies will fall before you by the sword.

So I will turn toward you and make you fruitful and multiply you, and I will confirm My covenant with you.

You will eat the old supply and clear out the old because of the new.

Moreover, I will make My dwelling among you, and My soul will not reject you.

I will also walk among you and be your God, and you shall be My people.

I am the Lord your God, who brought you out of the land of Egypt so that you would not be their slaves, and I broke the bars of your yoke and made you walk erect.

Leviticus 26:3-13 NASB

A tithe of everything from the land, whether grain from the soil or fruit from the trees, belongs to the Lord; it is holy to the Lord.

Whoever would redeem any of their tithe must add a fifth of the value to it.

Every tithe of the herd and flock—every tenth animal that passes under the shepherd's rod—will be holy to the Lord.

No one may pick out the good from the bad or make any substitution. If anyone does make a substitution, both the animal and its substitute become holy and cannot be redeemed.

These are the commands the Lord gave Moses at Mount Sinai for the Israelites.

Leviticus 27:30-34 NIV

'May the Lord bless you and protect you. May the Lord smile on you and be gracious to you. May the Lord show you his favor and give you his peace.'

Whenever Aaron and his sons bless the people of Israel in my name, I myself will bless them.

Numbers 6:24-27 NLT

If the Lord is pleased with us, he will lead us into that land and give us that fertile land.

Numbers 14:8 NCV

God is not a man, that he should lie; neither the son of man, that he should repent: hath he said, and shall he not do it? or hath he spoken, and shall he not make it good?

Behold, I have received commandment to bless: and he hath blessed; and I cannot reverse it.

Numbers 23: 19-20

See, I have given you this land, so go in and take it for yourselves. The Lord promised it to your ancestors—Abraham, Isaac, and Jacob and their descendants.

At that time I said, "I am not able to take care of you by myself. The LORD your God has made you grow in number so that there are as many of you as there are stars in the sky. I pray that the LORD, the God of your ancestors, will give you a thousand times more people and do all the wonderful things he promised.

Deuteronomy 1:8-11 NCV

For the Lord your God has blessed you in all the work of your hand. He knows your walking through this great wilderness. These forty years the Lord your God has been with you; you have lacked nothing.

Deuteronomy 2:7 AMP

Therefore know that the Lord your God, He is God, the faithful God who keeps covenant and mercy for a thousand generations with those who love Him and keep His commandments;

Deuteronomy 7:9 NKJV

Then it shall come to pass, because you listen to these judgments, and keep and do them, that the LORD your God will keep with you the covenant and the mercy which He swore to your fathers.

And He will love you and bless you and multiply you; He will also bless the fruit of your womb and the fruit of your land, your grain and your new wine and your oil, the increase of your cattle and the offspring of your flock, in the land of which He swore to your fathers to give you.

You shall be blessed above all peoples; there shall not be a male or female barren among you or among your livestock.

Deuteronomy 7:12-14 NKJV

Observe the commands of the Lord your God, walking in obedience to him and revering him. For the Lord your God is bringing you into a

good land—a land with brooks, streams, and
deep springs gushing out into the valleys and
hills; a land with wheat and barley, vines and fig
trees, pomegranates, olive oil and honey; a land
where bread will not be scarce and you will lack
nothing; a land where the rocks are iron and you
can dig copper out of the hills.

When you have eaten and are satisfied, praise
the Lord your God for the good land he has
given you. Be careful that you do not forget the
Lord your God, failing to observe his commands,
his laws and his decrees that I am giving you this
day. Otherwise, when you eat and are satisfied,
when you build fine houses and settle down, and
when your herds and flocks grow large and your

silver and gold increase and all you have is multiplied, then your heart will become proud and
you will forget the Lord your God, who brought

you out of Egypt, out of the land of slavery. He led you through the vast and dreadful wilderness, that thirsty and waterless land, with its venomous snakes and scorpions. He brought you water out of hard rock. He gave you manna to eat in the wilderness, something your ancestors had never known, to humble and test you so that in the end it might go well with you. You may say to yourself, "My power and the strength of my hands have produced this wealth for me." But remember the LORD your God, for it is he who gives you the ability to produce wealth, and so confirms his covenant, which he swore to your ancestors, as it is today.

Deuteronomy 8:6-18 NIV

So obey all the commands I am giving you today so that you will be strong and can go in and take the land you are going to take as your own.

Then you will live a long time in the land
that the Lord promised to give to your ancestors
and their descendants, a fertile land.

Deuteronomy 11:8-9 NCV

There, in the presence of the Lord your God,
you and your families shall eat and shall rejoice
in everything you have put your hand to, because
the Lord your God has blessed you.

Deuteronomy 12:7 NIV

You shall surely tithe all the produce from
what you sow, which comes out of the field every
year.

Deuteronomy 14:22 NASB

For the Lord thy God blesseth thee, as he
promised thee: and thou shalt lend unto many
nations, but thou shalt not borrow; and thou

shalt reign over many nations, but they shall not reign over thee.

If there be among you a poor man of one of thy brethren within any of thy gates in thy land which the LORD thy God giveth thee, thou shalt not harden thine heart, nor shut thine hand from thy poor brother:

But thou shalt open thine hand wide unto him, and shalt surely lend him sufficient for his need, in that which he wanteth.

Thou shalt surely give him, and thine heart shall not be grieved when thou givest unto him: because that for this thing the LORD thy God shall bless thee in all thy works, and in all that thou puttest thine hand unto.

For the poor shall never cease out of the land: therefore I command thee, saying, Thou shalt open thine hand wide unto thy brother, to thy poor, and to thy needy, in thy land.

Deuteronomy 15:6-8, 10, 11

Every man shall give as he is able, according to the blessing of the Lord thy God which he hath given thee.

Deuteronomy 16:17

When you make a vow to the Lord your God, you shall not delay to pay it, for it would be sin in you, and the Lord your God will surely require it of you.

However, if you refrain from vowing, it would not be sin in you.

You shall be careful to perform what goes out from your lips, just as you have voluntarily vowed to the Lord your God, what you have promised.

Deuteronomy 23:21-23 NASB

If you fully obey the Lord your God and carefully follow all his commands I give you today, the Lord your God will set you high above all the nations on earth. All these blessings will come on you and accompany you if you obey the Lord your God: You will be blessed in the city and blessed in the country. The fruit of your womb will be blessed, and the crops of your land and the young of your livestock—the calves of your herds and the lambs of your flocks.

Your basket and your kneading trough will be blessed. You will be blessed when you come in and blessed when you go out.

The Lord will grant that the enemies who rise up against you will be defeated before you. They will come at you from one direction but flee from you in seven.

The Lord will send a blessing on your barns and on everything you put your hand to. The

Lord your God will bless you in the land he is giving you.

The Lord will establish you as his holy people, as he promised you on oath, if you keep the commands of the Lord your God and walk in obedience to him. Then all the peoples on earth will see that you are called by the name of the Lord, and they will fear you. The Lord will grant you abundant prosperity—in the fruit of your womb, the young of your livestock and the crops of your ground—in the land he swore to your ancestors to give you.

The Lord will open the heavens, the storehouse of his bounty, to send rain on your land in season and to bless all the work of your hands. You will lend to many nations but will borrow from none. The Lord will make you the head, not the tail. If you pay attention to the commands of the Lord your God that I give you this day and carefully follow them, you will always be at the top, never at the bottom. Do not turn aside from any of the commands I give you today, to the right or to the left, following other gods and serving them.

Deuteronomy 28:1-14 NIV

Therefore, obey the terms of this covenant so that you will prosper in everything you do.

Deuteronomy 29:9 NLT

Then the Lord your God will make you most prosperous in all the work of your hands and in the fruit of your womb, the young of your livestock and the crops of your land. The Lord will again delight in you and make you prosperous, just as he delighted in your ancestors, if you obey the Lord your God and keep his commands and decrees that are written in this Book of the

Law and turn to the Lord your God with all your heart and with all your soul.

Deuteronomy 30:9-10 NIV

Look at what I've done for you today: I've placed in front of you Life and Good, Death and Evil. And I command you today: Love God, your God. Walk in his ways. Keep his commandments, regulations, and rules so that you will live, really live, live exuberantly, blessed by God, your God, in the land you are about to enter and possess.

Deuteronomy 30:15-16 MSG

I call heaven and earth to record this day against you, that I have set before you life and death, blessing and cursing: therefore choose life, that both thou and thy seed may live:

That thou mayest love the Lord thy God, and

that thou mayest obey his voice, and that thou mayest cleave unto him: for he is thy life, and the length of thy days: that thou mayest dwell in the land which the Lord sware unto thy fathers, to Abraham, to Isaac, and to Jacob, to give them.

Deuteronomy 30:19-20

I will give you every place where you set your foot, as I promised Moses.

Joshua 1:3 NIV

Only be strong and very courageous, that you may observe to do according to all the law which Moses My servant commanded you; do not turn from it to the right hand or to the left, that you may prosper wherever you go. This Book of the Law shall not depart from your mouth, but you shall meditate in it day and night, that you may observe to do according to all that is written in it. For then you will make your way prosperous, and then you will have good success.

Joshua 1:7-8 NKJV

The wife of a man from the company of the prophets cried out to Elisha, "Your servant my husband is dead, and you know that he revered the Lord. But now his creditor is coming to take my two boys as his slaves."

Elisha replied to her, "How can I help you? Tell me, what do you have in your house?"

"Your servant has nothing there at all," she said, "except a small jar of olive oil."

Elisha said, "Go around and ask all your neighbors for empty jars. Don't ask for just a few. Then go inside and shut the door behind you and your sons. Pour oil into all the jars, and as each is filled, put it to one side."

She left him and shut the door behind her and

her sons. They brought the jars to her and she kept pouring. When all the jars were full, she said to her son, "Bring me another one."

But he replied, "There is not a jar left." Then the oil stopped flowing.

She went and told the man of God, and he said, "Go, sell the oil and pay your debts.

You and your sons can live on what is left."

2 Kings 4:1-7 NIV

For you are God, O Lord. And you have promised these good things to your servant. And now, it has pleased you to bless the house of your servant, so that it will continue forever before you. For when you grant a blessing, O Lord, it is an eternal blessing!

1 Chronicles 17:26-27 NLT

Only the Lord give thee wisdom and understanding, and give thee charge concerning Israel,
that thou mayest keep the law of the Lord thy
God. Then shalt thou prosper, if thou takest heed
to fulfil the statutes and judgments which the
LORD charged Moses with concerning Israel:
be strong, and of good courage; dread not, nor
be dismayed.

1 Chronicles 22:12-13

Riches and honor come from you. You rule
everything. You have the power and strength to
make anyone great and strong.

1 Chronicles 29:12 NCV

And he died in a good old age, full of days,
riches, and honour.

1 Chronicles 29:28

Jehoshaphat had riches and honor in abundance.

2 Chronicles18:1 NKJV

Believe in the Lord your God, so shall ye be established; believe his prophets, so shall ye prosper.

2 Chronicles 20:20

And he did that which was right in the sight of the Lord, according to all that his father Amaziah did.

And he sought God in the days of Zechariah, who had understanding in the visions of God: and as long as he sought the Lord, God made him to prosper.

2 Chronicles 26:4-5

He ordered the people living in Jerusalem to give the portion due the priests and Levites so they could devote themselves to the Law of the Lord.

As soon as the order went out, the Israelites generously gave the firstfruits of their grain, new wine, olive oil and honey and all that the fields produced. They brought a great amount, a tithe of everything.

The people of Israel and Judah who lived in the towns of Judah also brought a tithe of their herds and flocks and a tithe of the holy things dedicated to the Lord their God, and they piled them in heaps.

They began doing this in the third month and finished in the seventh month.When Hezekiah and his officials came and saw the heaps, they praised the LORD and blessed his people Israel.

Hezekiah asked the priests and Levites about

the heaps; and Azariah the chief priest, from the family of Zadok, answered, "Since the people began to bring their contributions to the temple of the Lord, we have had enough to eat and plenty to spare, because the Lord has blessed his people, and this great amount is left over."

Hezekiah gave orders to prepare storerooms in the temple of the Lord, and this was done.

Then they faithfully brought in the contributions, tithes and dedicated gifts.

2 Chronicles 31:4-12 NIV

Thus Hezekiah did throughout all Judah, and he did what was good and right and true before the Lord his God. And in every work that he began in the service of the house of God, in the law and in the commandment, to seek his God, he did it with all his heart. So he prospered.

2 Chronicles 31:20-21 NKJV

I answered them, The God of heaven will prosper us; therefore we His servants will arise and build.

Nehemiah 2:20 AMP

"Indeed, forty years You provided for them in the wilderness and they were not in want; Their clothes did not wear out, nor did their feet swell.

"You also gave them kingdoms and peoples, And allotted them to them as a boundary. They took possession of the land of Sihon the king of Heshbon And the land of Og the king of Bashan.

"You made their sons numerous as the stars of heaven, And You brought them into the land which You had told their fathers to enter and possess.

"So their sons entered and possessed the land. And You subdued before them the inhabitants of the land, the Canaanites, And You gave them into their hand, with their kings and the peoples of the land, To do with them as they desired.

"They captured fortified cities and a fertile land. They took possession of houses full of every good thing, Hewn cisterns, vineyards, olive groves, Fruit trees in abundance. So they ate, were filled and grew fat, And reveled in Your great goodness."

Nehemiah 9:21-25 NASB

Your beginnings will seem humble, so prosperous will your future be.

Job 8:7 NIV

If they obey and serve him, they shall spend their days in prosperity, and their years in pleasures.

Job 36:11

The Lord blessed the latter part of Job's life more than the former part. He had fourteen thousand sheep, six thousand camels, a thousand yoke of oxen and a thousand donkeys. And he also had seven sons and three daughters.

After this, Job lived a hundred and forty years; he saw his children and their children to the fourth generation.

And so Job died, an old man and full of years.

Job 42: 12-13, 16, 17 NIV

Blessed is the man who walks not in the counsel of the ungodly, nor stands in the path of sinners, nor sits in the seat of the scornful;

But his delight is in the law of the LORD, and in His law he meditates day and night. He shall be like a tree planted by the rivers of water, that brings forth its fruit in its season, whose leaf also shall not wither; and whatever he does shall prosper.

Psalm 1:1-3 NKJV

May your blessing be on your people.

Psalm 3:8 NIV

For You, Lord, will bless the [uncompromisingly] righteous [him who is upright and in right standing with You]; as with a shield You will surround him with goodwill (pleasure and favor).

Psalm 5:12 AMP

The law of the Lord is perfect, restoring the [whole] person; the testimony of the Lord is sure, making wise the simple.

The precepts of the Lord are right, rejoicing the heart; the commandment of the Lord is pure and bright, enlightening the eyes.

The [reverent] fear of the Lord is clean, enduring forever; the ordinances of the Lord are true and righteous altogether.

More to be desired are they than gold, even than much fine gold; they are sweeter also than honey and drippings from the honeycomb.

Moreover, by them is Your servant warned (reminded, illuminated, and instructed); and in keeping them there is great reward.

Psalm 19:7-11 AMP

The Lord is my shepherd; I have all that I need.

He lets me rest in green meadows; he leads me beside peaceful streams.

He renews my strength. He guides me along right paths, bringing honor to his name.

Even when I walk through the darkest valley, I will not be afraid, for you are close beside me. Your rod and your staff protect and comfort me.

You prepare a feast for me in the presence of my enemies. You honor me by anointing my head with oil. My cup overflows with blessings.

Surely your goodness and unfailing love will pursue me all the days of my life, and I will live in the house of the Lord forever.

Psalm 23:1-6 NLT

Blessed is the nation whose God is the Lord; and the people whom he hath chosen for his own inheritance.

Psalm 33:12

The lions may grow weak and hungry, but those who seek the Lord lack no good thing.

Psalm 34:10 NIV

Even strong young lions sometimes go hungry, but those who trust in the Lord will lack no good thing.

Psalm 34:10 NLT

Let them shout for joy and rejoice, who favor my vindication; And let them say continually, "The Lord be magnified, Who delights in the prosperity of His servant."

Psalm 35:27 NASB

Day by day the Lord takes care of the innocent, and they will receive an inheritance

that lasts forever.

They will not be disgraced in hard times; even in famine they will have more than enough.

Psalm 37: 18-19 NLT

For such as be blessed of him shall inherit the earth.

Psalm 37:22

I have been young and now I am old. And in all my years I have never seen the Lord forsake a man who loves him; nor have I seen the children of the godly go hungry.

Instead, the godly are able to be generous with their gifts and loans to others, and their children are a blessing.

Psalm 37:25-26 TLB

For every beast of the forest is Mine, and the cattle upon a thousand hills or upon the mountains where thousands are.

Psalm 50:10 AMP

If riches increase, Do not set your heart on them.

Psalm 62:10b NKJV

You let people ride over our heads; we went through fire and water, but you brought us to a place of abundance.

Psalm 66:12 NIV

The land yields its harvest; God, our God, blesses us.

May God bless us still, so that all the ends of the earth will fear him.

Psalm 67:6-7 NIV

For the Lord God is a sun and shield: the Lord will give grace and glory: no good

thing will he withhold from them that walk uprightly.

Psalm 84:11

For Jehovah God is our Light and our Protector. He gives us grace and glory. No good thing will he withhold from those who walk along his paths.

O Lord of the armies of heaven, blessed are those who trust in you.

Psalm 84:11-12 TLB

Give to the Lord, O families of the peoples,
Give to the Lord glory and strength.

Give to the Lord the glory due His name;
Bring an offering, and come into His courts.

Psalm 96:7-8 NKJV

Give to the Lord, O families of the peoples,
Give to the Lord glory and strength.

Give to the Lord the glory due His name; Bring an offering, and come into His courts.

Psalm 104:24 NIV

And the Lord multiplied the people of Israel until they became too mighty for their enemies.

Psalm 105:24 NLT

Then he brought his people out, and they carried with them silver and gold. Not one of his people stumbled.

Psalm 105:37 NCV

Praise the Lord! Blessed is the man who fears the Lord, who delights greatly in His commandments.

His descendants will be mighty on earth; the generation of the upright will be blessed.

Wealth and riches will be in his house, and his righteousness endures forever.

Unto the upright there arises light in the darkness; He is gracious, and full of compassion, and righteous.

A good man deals graciously and lends; He will guide his affairs with discretion.

Psalm 112:1-5 NKJV

The Lord remembers us and will bless us: He will bless his people Israel, he will bless the house of Aaron,

he will bless those who fear the Lord— small and great alike.

May the Lord cause you to flourish, both you and your children.

May you be blessed by the Lord, the Maker of heaven and earth.

Psalm 115:12-15 NIV

Joyful are people of integrity, who follow the instructions of the Lord.

Joyful are those who obey his laws and search for him with all their hearts.

Psalm 119:1-2 NLT

Pray for the peace of Jerusalem: they shall prosper that love thee.

Peace be within thy walls, and prosperity within thy palaces.

Psalm 122:6-7

Blessed is every one who fears the Lord, who walks in His ways.

When you eat the labor of your hands, you shall be happy, and it shall be well with you.

Your wife shall be like a fruitful vine in the very heart of your house, your children like olive plants all around your table.

Behold, thus shall the man be blessed who fears the Lord.

The Lord bless you out of Zion, And may you see the good of Jerusalem all the days of your life.

Yes, may you see your children's children.

Peace be upon Israel!

Psalm 128:1-6 NKJV

I will bless her with abundant provisions; her poor I will satisfy with food.

Psalm 132:15 NIV

Honor the Lord with your wealth, with the firstfruits of all your crops; then your barns will be filled to overflowing, and your vats will brim over with new wine

Proverbs 3:9-10 NIV

Happy is the man who finds wisdom, and the man who gains understanding;

For her proceeds are better than the profits of silver, and her gain than fine gold.

She is more precious than rubies, and all the things you may desire cannot compare with her.

Length of days is in her right hand, in her left hand riches and honor.

Proverbs 3:13-16 NKJV

Do not withhold good from those who deserve it when it's in your power to help them.

If you can help your neighbor now, don't say, "Come back tomorrow, and then I'll help you."

Don't plot harm against your neighbor, for those who live nearby trust you.

The Lord curses the house of the wicked, but he blesses the home of the upright.

Proverbs 3:27-29, 33 NLT

You sleep a little; you take a nap. You fold your hands and lie down to rest.

So you will be as poor as if you had been robbed; you will have as little as if you had been held up.

Proverbs 6:10-11 NCV

Men do not despise a thief, if he steal to satisfy his soul when he is hungry;

But if he be found, he shall restore sevenfold; he shall give all the substance of his house.

Proverbs 6:30-31

Riches and honor are with me, enduring wealth and righteousness (uprightness in every area and relation, and right standing with God).

My fruit is better than gold, yes, than refined gold, and my increase than choice silver.

I [Wisdom] walk in the way of righteousness (moral and spiritual rectitude in every area and relation), in the midst of the paths of justice, that I may cause those who love me to inherit [true] riches and that I may fill their treasuries.

Proverbs 8:18-21 AMP

Now therefore listen to me, O you sons; for blessed (happy, fortunate, to be envied) are those who keep my ways.

Hear instruction and be wise, and do not refuse or neglect it.

Blessed (happy, fortunate, to be envied) is the man who listens to me, watching daily at my gates, waiting at the posts of my doors.

For whoever finds me [Wisdom] finds life and draws forth and obtains favor from the Lord.

Proverbs 8:32-35 AMP

The Lord does not let the righteous go hungry, but he thwarts the craving of the wicked.

Lazy hands make for poverty, but diligent hands bring wealth.

Proverbs 10:3-4 NIV

It is the blessing of the Lord that makes rich, and He adds no sorrow to it.

Proverbs 10:22 NASB

The desire of the righteous shall be granted.

Proverbs 10:24

There is one who scatters, and yet increases all the more, and there is one who withholds what is justly due, and yet it results only in want.

The generous man will be prosperous, and he who waters will himself be watered.

He who withholds grain, the people will curse him, but blessing will be on the head of him who sells it.

He who diligently seeks good seeks favor, But he who seeks evil, evil will come to him.

He who trusts in his riches will fall, but the righteous will flourish like the green leaf.

Proverbs 11:24-28 NASB

The soul of the sluggard desireth, and hath nothing: but the soul of the diligent shall be made fat.

Wealth gotten by vanity shall be diminished: but he that gathereth by labour shall increase.

Proverbs 13:4,11

Poverty and shame will come to him who disdains correction, but he who regards a rebuke will be honored.

Proverbs 13:18 NKJV

A good man leaveth an inheritance to his children's children: and the wealth of the sinner is laid up for the just.

Proverbs 13:22

The godly eat to their hearts' content, but the belly of the wicked goes hungry.

Proverbs 13:25 NLT

It is a sin to hate your neighbor, but being kind to the needy brings happiness

Proverbs 14:21 NCV

All hard work brings a profit, but mere talk leads only to poverty.

Proverbs 14:23 NIV

In the house of the righteous is much treasure: but in the revenues of the wicked is trouble.

Proverbs 15:6

The Lord will destroy the house of the proud: but he will establish the border of the widow.

Proverbs 15:25

But he who hates bribes will live.

Proverbs 15:27b NKJV

He who is slothful in his work Is a brother to him who is a great destroyer.

Proverbs 18:9 NKJV

House and riches are the inheritance of fathers: and a prudent wife is from the Lord.

Slothfulness casteth into a deep sleep; and an idle soul shall suffer hunger.

Proverbs 19:14-15

Whoever is kind to the poor lends to the Lord, and he will reward them for what they have done.

Proverbs 19:17 NIV

The fear of the Lord tendeth to life: and he that hath it shall abide satisfied; he shall not be visited with evil.

A slothful man hideth his hand in his bosom,

and will not so much as bring it to his mouth again.

Proverbs 19:23-24

The righteous lead blameless lives; blessed are their children after them.

Proverbs 20:7 NIV

Do not love sleep, lest you come to poverty;
Open your eyes, and you will be satisfied with bread.

Proverbs 20:13 NKJV

The thoughts of the diligent tend only to plenteousness; but of every one that is hasty only to want.

Proverbs 21:5

Whoever ignores the poor when they cry for help will also cry for help and not be answered.

Proverbs 21:13 NCV

He who loves pleasure will be a poor man; He who loves wine and oil will not be rich.

Proverbs 21:17 NKJV

The wise man saves for the future, but the foolish man spends whatever he gets.

Proverbs 21:20 TLB

A good name is rather to be chosen than great riches, and loving favor rather than silver and gold.

The rich and poor meet together; the Lord is the Maker of them all.

The reward of humility and the reverent and

worshipful fear of the Lord is riches and honor
and life.

Proverbs 22: 1-2, 4 AMP

The rich ruleth over the poor, and the bor-
rower is servant to the lender.

Proverbs 22:7

He that hath a bountiful eye shall be blessed;
for he giveth of his bread to the poor.

Proverbs 22:9

One who oppresses the poor to increase his
wealth and one who gives gifts to the rich—both
come to poverty.

Proverbs 22:16 NIV

Do you see someone skilled in their work?
They will serve before kings; they will not serve

before officials of low rank.

Proverbs 22:29 NIV

Don't weary yourself trying to get rich. Why waste your time? For riches can disappear as though they had the wings of a bird!

Proverbs 23:4-5 TLB

For the drunkard and the glutton will come to poverty, and drowsiness will clothe a man with rags.

Proverbs 23:21 NKJV

A house is built by wisdom and becomes strong through good sense. Through knowledge its rooms are filled with all sorts of precious riches and valuables.

Proverbs 24:3-4 NLT

I went by the field of the slothful, and by the vineyard of the man void of understanding;

And, lo, it was all grown over with thorns, and nettles had covered the face thereof, and the stone wall thereof was broken down.

Then I saw, and considered it well: I looked upon it, and received instruction.

Yet a little sleep, a little slumber, a little folding of the hands to sleep:

So shall thy poverty come as one that travelleth; and thy want as an armed man.

Proverbs 24:30-34

He that covereth his sins shall not prosper: but whoso confesseth and forsaketh them shall have mercy.

Proverbs 28:13

Hard work brings prosperity; playing around brings poverty.

The man who wants to do right will get a rich reward. But the man who wants to get rich quick will quickly fail.

Giving preferred treatment to rich people is a clear case of selling one's soul for a piece of bread.

Trying to get rich quick is evil and leads to poverty.

He who is of a greedy spirit stirs up strife, but he who puts his trust in the Lord shall be enriched and blessed.

Proverbs 28:19-22 TLB

The one who trusts the Lord will succeed.

Proverbs 28:25b NCV

Those who give to the poor will lack nothing,

but those who close their eyes to them receive many curses.

Proverbs 28:27 NIV

The king that faithfully judgeth the poor, his throne shall be established for ever.

Proverbs 29:14

That each of them may eat and drink, and find satisfaction in all their toil—this is the gift of God.

Ecclesiastes 3:13 NIV

Whoever loves money never has enough; whoever loves wealth is never satisfied with their income. This too is meaningless.

Ecclesiastes 5:10 NIV

Every man also to whom God hath given riches and wealth, and hath given him power to eat thereof, and to take his portion, and to rejoice in his labour; this is the gift of God.

Ecclesiastes 5:19

"If you become willing and obey me, you will eat good crops from the land.

But if you refuse to obey and if you turn against me, you will be destroyed by your enemies' swords." The Lord himself said these things.

Isaiah 1:19-20 NCV

He will also send you rain for the seed you sow in the ground, and the food that comes from the land will be rich and plentiful.

Isaiah 20:23

I give waters in the wilderness, and rivers in the desert, to give drink to my people, my chosen.

Isaiah 43:20b

I will go before you and make the crooked places straight; I will break in pieces the gates of bronze and cut the bars of iron.

I will give you the treasures of darkness and hidden riches of secret places, that you may know that I, the Lord, Who call you by your name, am the God of Israel.

Isaiah 45:2-3 NKJV

I, even I, have foretold it; yes, I have called him [Cyrus]; I have brought him, and [the Lord] shall make his way prosperous.

Isaiah 48:15 AMP

Thus saith the Lord, thy Redeemer, the Holy One of Israel; I am the Lord thy God which teacheth thee to profit, which leadeth thee by the way that thou shouldest go.

Isaiah 48:17

Is not this the kind of fasting I have chosen: to loose the chains of injustice and untie the cords of the yoke, to set the oppressed free and break every yoke?

Is it not to share your food with the hungry and to provide the poor wanderer with shelter— when you see the naked, to clothe them,

and not to turn away from your own flesh and blood?

Then your light will break forth like the dawn, and your healing will quickly appear; then your righteousness will go before you, and the glory of the Lord will be your rear guard.

Then you will call, and the Lord will answer; you will cry for help, and he will say: Here am I.

If you do away with the yoke of oppression, with the pointing finger and malicious talk,

and if you spend yourselves in behalf of the hungry and satisfy the needs of the oppressed, then your light will rise in the darkness, and your night will become like the noonday.

The Lord will guide you always; he will satisfy your needs in a sun-scorched land and will strengthen your frame. You will be like a well-watered garden, like a spring whose waters never fail.

Your people will rebuild the ancient ruins and will raise up the age-old foundations;

you will be called Repairer of Broken Walls, Restorer of Streets with Dwellings.

If you keep your feet from breaking the Sabbath and from doing as you please on my holy day, if you call the Sabbath a delight and the Lord's holy day honorable, and if you honor it by not going your own way and not doing as you please or speaking idle words, then you will find your joy in the Lord, and I will cause you to ride in triumph on the heights of the land and to feast on the inheritance of your father Jacob." For the mouth of the Lord has spoken.

Isaiah 58:6-14 NIV

Arise [from the depression and prostration in which circumstances have kept you—rise to a new life]! Shine (be radiant with the glory of the Lord), for your light has come, and the glory of the Lord has risen upon you!

For behold, darkness shall cover the earth, and

dense darkness [all] peoples, but the Lord shall arise upon you [O Jerusalem], and His glory shall be seen on you.

And nations shall come to your light, and kings to the brightness of your rising.

Then you shall see and be radiant, and your heart shall thrill and tremble with joy [at the glorious deliverance] and be enlarged; because the abundant wealth of the [Dead] Sea shall be turned to you, unto you shall the nations come with their treasures.

Isaiah 60:1-3,5 AMP

Unlike the past, invaders will not take their houses and confiscate their vineyards. For my people will live as long as trees, and my chosen ones will have time to enjoy their hard-won gains.

They will not work in vain, and their children will not be doomed to misfortune. For they are people blessed by the Lord, and their children, too, will be blessed.

Isaiah 65:22-23 NLT

Blessed is the man who trusts in the Lord, and whose hope is the Lord.

For he shall be like a tree planted by the waters, which spreads out its roots by the river, and will not fear when heat comes; But its leaf will be green, and will not be anxious in the year of drought, nor will cease from yielding fruit.

Jeremiah 17:7-8 NKJV

"He defended the cause of the poor and needy, and so all went well. Is that not what it means to know me?" declares the Lord.

Jeremiah 22:16 NIV

For I know the plans I have for you," declares the Lord, "plans to prosper you and not to harm you, plans to give you hope and a future.

Jeremiah 29:11 NIV

Behold, therefore, I beat My fists at the dishonest profit which you have made, and at the bloodshed which has been in your midst.

Ezekiel 22:13 NKJV

And you will live in Israel, the land I gave your ancestors long ago. You will be my people, and I will be your God.

I will cleanse you of your filthy behavior. I will give you good crops of grain, and I will send no more famines on the land.

I will give you great harvests from your fruit trees and fields, and never again will the sur rounding nations be able to scoff at your land for its famines.

Ezekiel 36:28-30 NLT

So be happy, people of Jerusalem; be joyful in the Lord your God. Because he does what is right, he has brought you rain; he has sent the fall rain and the spring rain for you, as before.

And the threshing floors will be full of grain; the barrels will overflow with new wine and olive oil.

Though I sent my great army against you— those swarming locusts and hopping locusts, the destroying locusts and the cutting locusts that ate your crops—I will pay you back for those years of trouble.

Then you will have plenty to eat and be full. You will praise the name of the Lord your God, who has done miracles for you. My people will never again be shamed.

Joel 2:23-26 NCV

For the seed shall be prosperous; the vine shall give her fruit, and the ground shall give her increase, and the heavens shall give their dew; and I will cause the remnant of this people to possess all these things.

Zechariah 8:12

Will a man rob God? Yet ye have robbed me. But ye say, Wherein have we robbed thee? In tithes and offerings.

Ye are cursed with a curse: for ye have robbed me, even this whole nation.

Bring ye all the tithes into the storehouse, that there may be meat in mine house, and prove me now herewith, saith the Lord of hosts, if I will not open you the windows of heaven, and pour you out a blessing, that there shall not be room enough to receive it.

And I will rebuke the devourer for your sakes, and he shall not destroy the fruits of your ground; neither shall your vine cast her fruit before the time in the field, saith the Lord of hosts.

And all nations shall call you blessed: for ye shall be a delightsome land, saith the Lord of hosts.

Malachi 3:8-12

New Testament

Thy kingdom come, Thy will be done in earth, as it is in heaven.

Give us this day our daily bread.

Matthew 6:10-11

Don't store up treasures here on earth, where moths eat them and rust destroys them, and where thieves break in and steal.

Store your treasures in heaven, where moths and rust cannot destroy, and thieves do not break in and steal.

Wherever your treasure is, there the desires of your heart will also be.

Matthew 6:19-21 NLT

Therefore I say to you, do not worry about your life, what you will eat or what you will

drink; nor about your body, what you will put on. Is not life more than food and the body more than clothing?

Look at the birds of the air, for they neither sow nor reap nor gather into barns; yet your heavenly Father feeds them. Are you not of more value than they?

Which of you by worrying can add one cubit to his stature?

So why do you worry about clothing? Consider the lilies of the field, how they grow: they neither toil nor spin; and yet I say to you that even Solomon in all his glory was not arrayed like one of these.

Now if God so clothes the grass of the field, which today is, and tomorrow is thrown into the oven, will He not much more clothe you, O you of little faith?

Therefore do not worry, saying, 'What shall we eat?' or 'What shall we drink?' or 'What shall we wear?'

For after all these things the Gentiles seek. For your heavenly Father knows that you need all these things.

But seek first the kingdom of God and His righteousness, and all these things shall be added to you.

Matthew 6:25-33 NKJV

But the seed falling on good soil refers to someone who hears the word and understands it. This is the one who produces a crop, yielding a hundred, sixty or thirty times what was sown.

Matthew 13:23 NIV

Then when they arrived at Capernaum the Temple tax-collectors came up and said to Peter, "Your master doesn't pay Temple-tax, we presume?"

"Oh, yes, he does!" replied Peter. Later when he went into the house Jesus anticipated what he was going to say. "What do you think, Simon?" he said. "Whom do the kings of this world get their rates and taxes from—their own people or from others?"

"From others," replied Peter.

"Then the family is exempt," Jesus told him. "Yet we don't want to give offence to these people, so go down to the lake and throw in your hook. Take the first fish that bites, open his mouth and you'll find a coin. Take that and give it to them, for both of us."

Matthew 17:24-27 Phillips

In that way the kingdom of heaven is like this. A king was ready to finish his business with his servants.

The first servant was brought in. He owed the king a very large sum of money.

He could not pay it. So his master said, "Go sell him, his wife, his children, and everything he has, and pay me!"

So the servant bowed down in front of him. He begged, "Sir, give me time. I will pay everything."

His master was sorry for him and let him go. He did not make him pay the money.

That same servant went out and met another servant. This man owed him a much smaller sum of money. He caught him by the throat and said, "Pay me what you owe me!"

Then this servant bowed down in front of him. He begged, "Give me time. I will pay you."

But he said, "No." He went and put the man in prison until he could pay what he owed him.

The other servants saw what he did. They were very sad. They went and told their master everything that had been done.

Then his master called the first servant to him. He said, "You bad man! I let you go. I did not make you pay all you owed me, because you begged me to be kind to you.

You should have been kind to the other servant, as I was kind to you."

His master was very angry. He turned the servant over to the prison guards until he could pay all he owed him.

That is like what my Father in heaven will do to every one of you, if you do not forgive your brother from your heart.

Matthew 18:23-35 WE

A man came to Jesus and asked, "Teacher, what good thing must I do to have life forever?"

Jesus answered, "Why do you ask me about what is good? Only God is good. But if you want to have life forever, obey the commands."

The man asked, "Which commands?"

Jesus answered, "You must not murder anyone; you must not be guilty of adultery; you must not steal; you must not tell lies about your neighbor; honor your father and mother; and love your neighbor as you love yourself."

The young man said, "I have obeyed all these things. What else do I need to do?"

Jesus answered, "If you want to be perfect, then go and sell your possessions and give the money to the poor. If you do this, you will have treasure in heaven. Then come and follow me."

But when the young man heard this, he left

sorrowfully, because he was rich.

Then Jesus said to his followers, "I tell you the truth, it will be hard for a rich person to enter the kingdom of heaven.

Yes, I tell you that it is easier for a camel to go through the eye of a needle than for a rich person to enter the kingdom of God."

When Jesus' followers heard this, they were very surprised and asked, "Then who can be saved?"

Jesus looked at them and said, "For people this is impossible, but for God all things are possible."

Matthew 19:16-26 NCV

For the kingdom of heaven is like a man traveling to a far country, who called his own servants and delivered his goods to them.

And to one he gave five talents, to another two,

and to another one, to each according to his own ability; and immediately he went on a journey.

Then he who had received the five talents went and traded with them, and made another five talents.

And likewise he who had received two gained two more also.

But he who had received one went and dug in the ground, and hid his lord's money.

After a long time the lord of those servants came and settled accounts with them.

So he who had received five talents came and brought five other talents, saying, 'Lord, you delivered to me five talents; look, I have gained five more talents besides them.'

His lord said to him, 'Well done, good and faithful servant; you were faithful over a few things, I will make you ruler over many things. Enter into the joy of your lord.'

He also who had received two talents came and said, 'Lord, you delivered to me two talents; look, I have gained two more talents besides them.'

His lord said to him, 'Well done, good and faithful servant; you have been faithful over a few things, I will make you ruler over many things. Enter into the joy of your lord.'

Then he who had received the one talent came and said, 'Lord, I knew you to be a hard man, reaping where you have not sown, and gathering where you have not scattered seed.

And I was afraid, and went and hid your talent in the ground. Look, there you have what is yours.'

But his lord answered and said to him, 'You wicked and lazy servant, you knew that I reap where I have not sown, and gather where I have not scattered seed. So you ought to have deposited my money with the bankers, and at my coming I would have received back my own with interest.

Therefore take the talent from him, and give it to him who has ten talents. For to everyone who has, more will be given, and he will have abundance; but from him who does not have, even what he has will be taken away.'

Matthew 25:14-29 NKJV

But they think about the things of this world. They want to get money and other things to be happy. These things push the message out of their hearts. No good comes from it.

Mark 4:19 WE

And Jesus answered and said, Verily I say unto you, There is no man that hath left house, or brethren, or sisters, or father, or mother, or wife, or children, or lands, for my sake, and the gospel's, but he shall receive an hundredfold now in this time, houses, and brethren, and sisters, and mothers, and children, and lands, with persecutions; and in the world to come eternal life.

Mark 10:29-30

"Have faith in God," Jesus answered. "Truly I tell you, if anyone says to this mountain, 'Go, throw yourself into the sea,' and does not doubt in their heart but believes that what they say will happen, it will be done for them. Therefore I tell you, whatever you ask for in prayer, believe that

you have received it, and it will be yours."

Mark 11:22-24 NIV

Jesus sat down in the temple near the place where people put in their money. He saw how the people put in money. Many rich people put in much money.

A poor woman, whose husband was dead, came. She put in two small pieces of money.

Jesus called his disciples. He said, `I tell you the truth. This poor woman has given more money than all the other people.

All these people had plenty of money and they gave only a part of it. She was poor and she gave everything she had. She has nothing left to live on.'

Mark 12:41-44 WE

One day the people were crowding closely round Jesus to hear God's message, as he stood on the shore of Lake Gennesaret. Jesus noticed two boats drawn up on the beach, for the fishermen had left them there while they were cleaning their nets. He went aboard one of the boats, which belonged to Simon, and asked him to push out a little from the shore. Then he sat down and continued his teaching of the crowds from the boat.

When he had finished speaking, he said to Simon, "Push out now into deep water and let down your nets for a catch."

Simon replied, "Master! We've worked all night and never caught a thing, but if you say so, I'll let the nets down."

And when they had done this, they caught an enormous shoal of fish—so big that the nets began to tear. So they signalled to their friends in the other boats to come and help them. They came and filled both the boats to sinking point.

Luke 5:1-7 Phillips

Give and men will give to you—yes, good measure, pressed down, shaken together and running over will they pour into your lap. For whatever measure you use with other people, they will use in their dealings with you."

Luke 6:38 Phillips

Then Jesus answered and said: "A certain man went down from Jerusalem to Jericho, and fell among thieves, who stripped him of his clothing, wounded him, and departed, leaving him half dead.

"Now by chance a certain priest came down that road. And when he saw him, he passed by on the other side.

"Likewise a Levite, when he arrived at the place, came and looked, and passed by on the other side.

"But a certain Samaritan, as he journeyed,

came where he was. And when he saw him, he had compassion.

"So he went to him and bandaged his wounds, pouring on oil and wine; and he set him on his own animal, brought him to an inn, and took care of him.

"On the next day, when he departed, he took out two denarii, gave them to the innkeeper, and said to him, 'Take care of him; and whatever more you spend, when I come again, I will repay you.'

"So which of these three do you think was neighbor to him who fell among the thieves?"

And he said, "He who showed mercy on him."

Then Jesus said to him, "Go and do likewise."

Luke 10:30-37 NKJV

What sorrow awaits you Pharisees! For you are careful to tithe even the tiniest income from your herb gardens, but you ignore justice and the love of God. You should tithe, yes, but do not neglect the more important things.

Luke 11:42 NLT

Then he said to them, "Watch out! Be on your guard against all kinds of greed; life does not consist in an abundance of possessions."

And he told them this parable: "The ground of a certain rich man yielded an abundant harvest.

He thought to himself, 'What shall I do? I have no place to store my crops.'

"Then he said, 'This is what I'll do. I will tear down my barns and build bigger ones, and there I will store my surplus grain.

And I'll say to myself, "You have plenty of grain laid up for many years. Take life easy; eat, drink and be merry."'

"But God said to him, 'You fool! This very

night your life will be demanded from you. Then who will get what you have prepared for yourself?'

"This is how it will be with whoever stores up things for themselves but is not rich toward God."

Luke 12:15-21 NIV

So Jesus, raising his eyes and seeing a great crowd on the way towards him, said to Philip, "Where can we buy food for these people to eat?" (He said this to test Philip, for he himself knew what he was going to do.)

"Ten pounds' worth of bread would not be enough for them," Philip replied, "even if they had only a little each."

Then Andrew, Simon Peter's brother, another disciple, put in, "There is a boy here who has five small barley loaves and a couple of fish, but what's the good of that for such a crowd?"

Then Jesus said, "Get the people to sit down."

There was plenty of grass there, and the men, some five thousand of them, sat down. Then Jesus took the loaves, gave thanks for them and distributed them to the people sitting on the grass, and he distributed the fish in the same way, giving them as much as they wanted. When they had eaten enough, Jesus said to his disciples, "Collect the pieces that are left over so that nothing is wasted."

So they did as he suggested and filled twelve baskets with the broken pieces of the five barley loaves, which were left over after the people had eaten!

John 6:5-13 Phillips

A thief is only there to steal and kill and destroy. I came so they can have real and eternal life, more and better life than they ever dreamed of.

John 10:10 MSG

Afterward Jesus appeared again to his disciples, by the Sea of Galilee. It happened this way: Simon Peter, Thomas (also known as Didymus), Nathanael from Cana in Galilee, the sons of Zebedee, and two other disciples were together. "I'm going out to fish," Simon Peter told them, and they said, "We'll go with you." So they went out and got into the boat, but that night they caught nothing.

Early in the morning, Jesus stood on the shore, but the disciples did not realize that it was Jesus.

He called out to them, "Friends, haven't you any fish?"

"No," they answered.

He said, "Throw your net on the right side of the boat and you will find some." When they did, they were unable to haul the net in because of the large number of fish.

Then the disciple whom Jesus loved said to Peter, "It is the Lord!" As soon as Simon Peter heard him say, "It is the Lord," he wrapped his outer garment around him (for he had taken it off) and jumped into the water. The other disciples followed in the boat, towing the net full of fish, for they were not far from shore, about a hundred yards. When they landed, they saw a fire of burning coals there with fish on it, and some bread.

Jesus said to them, "Bring some of the fish you have just caught."

So Simon Peter climbed back into the boat and dragged the net ashore. It was full of large fish,

153, but even with so many the net was not torn. Jesus said to them, "Come and have breakfast." None of the disciples dared ask him, "Who are you?" They knew it was the Lord. Jesus came, took the bread and gave it to them, and did the same with the fish. This was now the third time Jesus appeared to his disciples after he was raised from the dead.

John 21:1-14 NIV

And with great power the apostles gave witness to the resurrection of the Lord Jesus. And great grace was upon them all. Nor was there anyone among them who lacked; for all who were possessors of lands or houses sold them, and brought the proceeds of the things that were sold, and laid them at the apostles' feet; and they distributed to each as anyone had need.

And Joses, who was also named Barnabas by

the apostles (which is translated Son of Encouragement), a Levite of the country of Cyprus, having land, sold it, and brought the money and laid it at the apostles' feet.

Acts 4:33-37 NKJV

At Caesarea there was a man named Cornelius, a centurion in what was known as the Italian Regiment. He and all his family were devout and God-fearing; he gave generously to those in need and prayed to God regularly. One day at about three in the afternoon he had a vision. He distinctly saw an angel of God, who came to him and said, "Cornelius!"

Cornelius stared at him in fear. "What is it, Lord?" he asked.

The angel answered, "Your prayers and gifts to the poor have come up as a memorial offering before God."

Acts 10: 1-4 NIV

And now, brethren, I commend you to God, and to the word of his grace, which is able to build you up, and to give you an inheritance among all them which are sanctified.

I have coveted no man's silver, or gold, or apparel. Yea, ye yourselves know, that these hands have ministered unto my necessities, and to them that were with me.

I have shewed you all things, how that so labouring ye ought to support the weak, and to remember the words of the Lord Jesus, how he said, It is more blessed to give than to receive.

Acts 20:32-35

The holy writings say, "No eye has seen the things God has made ready for those who love him. No ear has heard about them. No person's heart has ever thought of them."

1 Corinthians 2:9 WE

On the first [day] of each week, let each one of you [personally] put aside something and save it up as he has prospered [in proportion to what he is given], so that no collections will need to be taken after I come.

And when I arrive, I will send on those whom you approve and authorize with credentials to carry your gift [of charity] to Jerusalem.

1 Corinthians 16:2-3 AMP

But this I say, He which soweth sparingly shall reap also sparingly; and he which soweth bountifully shall reap also bountifully.

Every man according as he purposeth in his heart, so let him give; not grudgingly, or of necessity: for God loveth a cheerful giver.

And God is able to make all grace abound toward you; that ye, always having all sufficiency in all things, may abound to every good work:

(As it is written, He hath dispersed abroad; he hath given to the poor: his righteousness remaineth for ever. Now he that ministereth seed to the sower both minister bread for your food, and multiply your seed sown, and increase the fruits of your righteousness;)

Being enriched in every thing to all bountifulness, which causeth through us thanksgiving to God.

For the administration of this service not only supplieth the want of the saints, but is abundant also by many thanksgivings unto God;

2 Corinthians 9:6-12

So all who put their faith in Christ share the same blessing Abraham received because of his faith.

But those who depend on the law to make them right with God are under his curse, for the

Scriptures say, "Cursed is everyone who does not observe and obey all the commands that are written in God's Book of the Law." So it is clear that no one can be made right with God by trying to keep the law. For the Scriptures say, "It is through faith that a righteous person has life." This way of faith is very different from the way of law, which says, "It is through obeying the law that a person has life." But Christ has rescued us from the curse pronounced by the law. When he was hung on the cross, he took upon himself the curse for our wrongdoing. For it is written in the Scriptures, "Cursed is everyone who is hung on a tree." Through Christ Jesus, God has blessed the Gentiles with the same blessing he promised to Abraham, so that we who are believers might receive the promised Holy Spirit through faith.

And now that you belong to Christ, you are the true children of Abraham. You are his heirs, and

God's promise to Abraham belongs to you.

Galatians 3:9-14, 29 NLT

Do not be fooled: You cannot cheat God. People harvest only what they plant. If they plant to satisfy their sinful selves, their sinful selves will bring them ruin. But if they plant to please the Spirit, they will receive eternal life from the Spirit. We must not become tired of doing good.

We will receive our harvest of eternal life at the right time if we do not give up. When we have the opportunity to help anyone, we should do it. But we should give special attention to those who are in the family of believers.

Galatians 6:7-10 NCV

Let him that stole steal no more: but rather let him labour, working with his hands the thing which is good, that he may have to give to him that needeth.

Ephesians 4:28

I rejoiced greatly in the Lord that at last you renewed your concern for me. Indeed, you were concerned, but you had no opportunity to show it.

I am not saying this because I am in need, for I have learned to be content whatever the circumstances. I know what it is to be in need, and I know what it is to have plenty. I have learned the secret of being content in any and every situation, whether well fed or hungry, whether living in plenty or in want.

I can do all this through him who gives me strength.

Yet it was good of you to share in my troubles.

Moreover, as you Philippians know, in the early

days of your acquaintance with the gospel, when I set out from Macedonia, not one church shared with me in the matter of giving and receiving, except you only; for even when I was in Thessalonica, you sent me aid more than once when I was in need.

Not that I desire your gifts; what I desire is that more be credited to your account.

I have received full payment and have more than enough. I am amply supplied, now that I have received from Epaphroditus the gifts you sent. They are a fragrant offering, an acceptable sacrifice, pleasing to God.

And my God will meet all your needs according to the riches of his glory in Christ Jesus.

Philippians 4:10-19 NIV

Brothers and sisters, by the authority of our Lord Jesus Christ we command you to stay away from any believer who refuses to work and does not follow the teaching we gave you.

You yourselves know that you should live as we live. We were not lazy when we were with you.

And when we ate another person's food, we always paid for it. We worked very hard night and day so we would not be an expense to any of you. We had the right to ask you to help us, but we worked to take care of ourselves so we would be an example for you to follow.

When we were with you, we gave you this rule: "Anyone who refuses to work should not eat."

We hear that some people in your group refuse to work. They do nothing but busy themselves in other people's lives.

We command those people and beg them in the Lord Jesus Christ to work quietly and earn their own food.

2 Thessalonians 3:6-12 NCV

But if anyone does not provide for his own, and especially for those of his household, he has denied the faith and is worse than an unbeliever.

1 Timothy 5:8 NKJV

But godliness with contentment is great gain. For we brought nothing into the world, and we can take nothing out of it. But if we have food and clothing, we will be content with that.

Those who want to get rich fall into temptation and a trap and into many foolish and harmful desires that plunge people into ruin and destruction.

For the love of money is a root of all kinds of evil. Some people, eager for money, have wandered from the faith and pierced themselves with many griefs.

1 Timothy 6:6-10 NIV

Command those who are rich in this present world not to be arrogant nor to put their hope in wealth, which is so uncertain, but to put their hope in God, who richly provides us with everything for our enjoyment. Command them to do good, to be rich in good deeds, and to be generous and willing to share. In this way they will lay up treasure for themselves as a firm foundation for the coming age, so that they may take hold of the life that is truly life.

1 Timothy 6:17-19 NIV

For this Melchizedek, king of Salem, priest of the Most High God, who met Abraham returning from the slaughter of the kings and blessed him, to whom also Abraham gave a tenth part of all, first being translated "king of righteousness," and then also king of Salem, meaning "king of peace," without father, without mother, without genealogy, having neither beginning of days nor end of life, but made like the Son of God, remains a priest continually.

Now consider how great this man was, to whom even the patriarch Abraham gave a tenth of the spoils.

And indeed those who are of the sons of Levi, who receive the priesthood, have a commandment to receive tithes from the people according to the law, that is, from their brethren, though they have come from the loins of Abraham; but he whose genealogy is not derived from them received tithes from Abraham and blessed him who had the promises.

Now beyond all contradiction the lesser is blessed by the better.

Here mortal men receive tithes, but there he receives them, of whom it is witnessed that he lives. For it is evident that our Lord arose from

Judah, of which tribe Moses spoke nothing concerning priesthood.

And it is yet far more evident if, in the likeness of Melchizedek, there arises another priest who has come, not according to the law of a fleshly commandment, but according to the power of an endless life. By so much more Jesus has become a surety of a better covenant.

Hebrews 7:1-8, 14-16, 22 NKJV

Beloved, I wish above all things that thou mayest prosper and be in health, even as thy soul prospereth.

3 John 2

After this I looked, and, behold, a door was opened in heaven: and the first voice which I heard was as it were of a trumpet talking with me; which said, Come up hither, and I will shew thee things which must be hereafter.

And immediately I was in the spirit: and, behold, a throne was set in heaven, and one sat on the throne.

And he that sat was to look upon like a jasper and a sardine stone: and there was a rainbow round about the throne, in sight like unto an emerald.

And round about the throne were four and twenty seats: and upon the seats I saw four and twenty elders sitting, clothed in white raiment; and they had on their heads crowns of gold.

Revelation 4:1-4

He who overcomes shall inherit all things, and I will be his God and he shall be My son.

Revelation 21:7 NKJV

The wall was made of jasper, and the city was pure gold, as clear as glass.

The wall of the city was built on foundation stones inlaid with twelve precious stones: the first was jasper, the second sapphire, the third agate, the fourth emerald,

the fifth onyx, the sixth carnelian, the seventh chrysolite, the eighth beryl, the ninth topaz,

the tenth chrysoprase, the eleventh jacinth, the twelfth amethyst.

The twelve gates were made of pearls—each gate from a single pearl! And the main street was pure gold, as clear as glass.

Revelation 21:18-21 NLT

Look, I am coming soon! My reward is with me, and I will give to each person according to what they have done.

I am the Alpha and the Omega, the First and

the Last, the Beginning and the End.

Blessed are those who wash their robes, that they may have the right to the tree of life and may go through the gates into the city.

Revelation 22:12-14 NIV

PRAYER OF SALVATION

God loves you—no matter who you are, no matter what your past. God loves you so much that He gave His one and only begotten Son for you. The Bible tells us that "...whoever believes in Him shall not perish but have eternal life" (John 3:16 NIV). Jesus laid down His life and rose again so that we could spend eternity with Him in heaven and experience His absolute best on earth. If you would like to receive Jesus into your life, say the following prayer out loud and mean it from your heart.

> *Heavenly Father, I come to You admitting that I am a sinner. Right now, I choose to turn away from sin, and I ask You to cleanse me of all unrighteousness. I believe that Your Son, Jesus, died on the cross to take away my sins. I also believe that He rose again from the dead so that I might be forgiven of my sins and made righteous through faith in Him. I call upon the name of Jesus Christ to be the Savior and Lord of my life. Jesus, I choose to follow You and ask that You fill me with the power of the Holy Spirit. I declare that right now I am a child of God. I am free from sin and full of the righteousness of God. I am saved in Jesus' name. Amen.*

If you prayed this prayer to receive Jesus Christ as your Savior for the first time, please contact us on the Web at **www.harrisonhouse.com** to receive a free book.

Or you may write to us at

Harrison House • P.O. Box 35035 • Tulsa, Oklahoma 74153

Fast. Easy.
Convenient.

For the latest Harrison House product information and author news, look no further than your computer. All the details on our powerful, life-changing products are just a click away. New releases, E-mail subscriptions, testimonies, monthly specials—find it all in one place. Visit harrisonhouse.com today!

harrisonhouse

The Harrison House Vision

Proclaiming the truth and the power

Of the Gospel of Jesus Christ

With excellence;

Challenging Christians to

Live victoriously,

Grow spiritually,

Know God intimately.